The Generation
of Caliban

THE 2001 GARNETT SEDGEWICK

MEMORIAL LECTURE

⎯ᗡ

Jonathan Goldberg

RONSDALE PRESS

VANCOUVER

THE GENERATION OF CALIBAN
Copyright © 2002 Jonathan Goldberg

Ronsdale Press
3350 West 21st Avenue
Vancouver, B.C., Canada
V6S 1G7

Set in Minion: 11 on 15
Typesetting: Julie Cochrane
Printing: The Printing House Ltd., Vancouver, B.C.
Cover Design: Julie Cochrane
Author Photo Credit: Duke University Photography, photo by Jim Wallace

Ronsdale Press wishes to thank the Canada Council for the Arts, the Government of Canada through the Book Publishing Industry Development Program (BPIDP), and the Province of British Columbia through the British Columbia Arts Council for their support of its publishing program.

National Library of Canada Cataloguing in Publication Data

Goldberg, Jonathan.
  The generation of Caliban

ISBN 0-921870-93-0

1. Caliban (Fictitious character) 2. Shakespeare, William, 1564–1616 — Characters — Caliban. 3. Shakespeare, William, 1564–1616. Tempest. 4. Lamming, George, 1927– Pleasures of exile. I. Title.
PR2833.G64 2002   822.3'3   C2001-911285-8

ACKNOWLEDGEMENTS

My thanks to Adam Frank, for suggesting that I visit UBC; to Sherrill E. Grace, for inviting me to deliver the Garnett Sedgewick Memorial Lecture; to Laurie Ricou, for making the arrangements; to Ron Hatch, for overseeing its printing; to Margery Fee, for sharing her work with me; and to Paul Yachnin, for his engagement.

INTRODUCTION — SEDGEWICK
MEMORIAL LECTURE, 20 MARCH 2001

The Sedgewick Lecture is named in honour of Garnett G. Sedgewick, who was the first Head of the Department of English, and the first lecture was given in 1955 (six years after his death). Over the years, many distinguished scholars and writers have given the Sedgewick Lecture — Robert Heilman, Harry Levin, Hugh MacLennan, Northrop Frye, Robert Bringhurst, and Sandra Djwa, to name a few.

This year's Sedgewick Lecturer is Dr. Jonathan Goldberg, Sir William Osler Professor of English Literature at Johns Hopkins University. Dr. Goldberg is a specialist in the English Renaissance with books on Spenser, Shakespeare and his contemporaries, Milton, and on a wide range of social, political, and cultural aspects of the period. *The Generation of Caliban* marks an ideal conjunction of scholarly interests, and its presentation at UBC in the series that honours Dr. Sedgewick is especially appropriate. In this lecture Dr. Goldberg, while returning to his first love — Shakespeare — is placing *The Tempest* in a modern, indeed a *postmodern* setting by reading the play through the colonial and national lenses of the great Barbadian writer George Lamming. He is viewing the *old* world author through a *new* world optic, which permits us to see both Lamming and ourselves in new ways. This bringing of the bard to the so-called *new* world was a passion of Sedgewick's; *he* saw Shakespeare as always relevant, as belonging here on the west coast as much as anywhere. With Vancouver's "Bard on the Beach" summer festival and with John Juliani's "Savage God" readings of the plays, both of which are regular, continuing, favourites with Vancouver audiences, time has proven Garnett Sedgewick right.

In *The Generation of Caliban,* which will form part of his new book on *The Tempest,* Jonathan Goldberg continues the Sedgewick tradition (although he has added splendid visuals to the verbal record), and I can imagine our former Head applauding what Goldberg does with the play.

The Department of English's annual Sedgewick Lectures, now published by Ronsdale Press, has established its own tradition to which the 2001 lecture is an outstanding contribution. Dr. Goldberg had a large, diverse, and interested audience for his talk and the questions afterwards were lively and provocative. It is on such occasions that we gather to celebrate not only the past but the future richness and vitality of the Humanities within and beyond the academy.

Sherrill E. Grace
Professor and Head

THE GENERATION
OF CALIBAN

This essay is part of a larger project on Shakespeare's *Tempest* on which I am currently engaged, a portion of which has appeared in an essay that begins the work of reading Shakespeare's play for the ways in which Sycorax the witch and her monstrous mooncalf son Caliban, whose father may be the devil, call up the spectre of transgression that goes by the name of "sodomy" in the Elizabethan age.[1] I will not have much to say about *The Tempest* here, however, although questions of sexuality will play a part in the discussion that follows. My broadest concerns in this essay develop what is generally acknowledged as the prevailing view in readings of this play by those practitioners in Renaissance studies usually termed New Historicists, an insistence on understanding Shakespeare's play as shaped by, and as a contributor to and participant in the discourses of colonialism.[2] In advancing these arguments, I am particularly inspired by a body of criticism which has only recently been noticed by Renaissance scholars — readings of *The Tempest* launched by those involved in colonial struggle and resistance.[3] While New Historicist readings of *The Tempest* began some twenty-five years ago, these interventions — by Caribbean and Latin American writers most notably — have a history stretching back to the beginning of the twentieth century.

In the history of appropriations of the play for colonial/nationalist uses, the Barbadian novelist and critic George Lamming has been credited by Roberto Fernández Retamar (in his 1971 manifesto "Caliban: Notes Toward a Discussion of Culture in Our America") as "the first writer in our world to assume our identification with Caliban."[4] Lamming does this in his 1960 *The Pleasures of Exile,* a collection of political essays in which the relationship of Prospero and Caliban is used throughout as a shorthand for the relationship of colonizer to colonized, and in which the proposition that "Caliban Orders History" (to cite a chapter title) is developed.[5] Lamming's work is significant not merely as the initiator of a contestatory position of analysis; *The Pleasures of Exile* is further remarkable among the texts that deploy the trope of the relationship of Caliban and Prospero in that it devotes a full chapter to a reading of *The Tempest.* Lamming's analysis indicates the belatedness of New Historicist interpretations of the play. Moreover, his work — as well as interventions which follow it — provides a number of terms of analysis that go much further than New Historicist inquiry, and which further the impetus for my own project.

Lamming's reading of *The Tempest* takes as one focus the same subject that Stephen Greenblatt addressed in his 1976 essay "Learning to Curse: Aspects of Linguistic Colonialism in the Sixteenth Century," an essay that can perhaps stand to mark a significant beginning to the New Historicist tradition of reading the play within the history of colonization.[6] For Lamming as for Greenblatt the question of linguistic colonization is crucial. Here is Lamming:

> Prospero has given Caliban Language; and with it an unstated history of consequences, an unknown history of future intentions. This gift of Language meant not English, in particular, but speech and concept as a way, a method, a necessary avenue towards areas of the self which could not be reached in any other way. It is this way, entirely Prospero's enterprise, which makes Caliban aware of possibilities. Therefore, all of Caliban's future — for future is the very name for possibilities — must derive from Prospero's experiment which is also his risk. (*Pleasures of Exile* 109)

For Greenblatt, linguistic colonization basically has two aspects: either the native is regarded as having no language or it is assumed that the native is transparent and totally available to be

Portrait of George Lamming by Denis Williams, frontispiece
to In the Castle of My Skin *(1953)*

known and dominated. Either way, the native is regarded as virtually innocent and resourceless and the imposition of a foreign tongue is taken to be an ultimate violation from which there is no hope of recovery; indeed, Greenblatt goes so far as to write that "the primal crime in the New World was committed in the interest of language" [563]. Like the well-known scene in Lévi-Strauss critiqued by Derrida in *Of Grammatology,* Greenblatt's story is open to charges of an idealism that "salvages" native culture in several senses of the word, the most pertinent being a refusal to grant to

native societies either the full sociality of western ones or any futurity. Greenblatt thus ends his essay mourning that "the people of
the New World will never speak to us," claiming that they are "lost
to us forever" (576). Through the figure of Caliban, Greenblatt sees
the native ability to hold on to a shred of what he calls his "human
pain" (570) only by using the language imposed on him as a tool
with which to curse his oppressor, but he also finds that Shakespeare allows Caliban a density in his poetic utterances that testifies
to a valued metaphoricity of language. This grants to Shakespearian
representation the very quality of a universalizing knowledge that
elsewhere Greenblatt critiques as a tool of colonial misrecognition.
This too can be seen as an idealistic gesture, one that has been effec-
tively displaced in later historicizing essays, most notably in Paul
Brown's argument that Caliban's poetry of resignation to his en-
slavement, waking only to dream again, serves not as a sign of
human liberation but of further colonization.[7]

Lamming, writing, as Retamar suggests, in a position of identification with Caliban, presents an argument that bears compari-
son with Greenblatt's, but which also departs significantly from it.
It differs most forcibly in regarding language as a tool of advance-
ment. Lamming notes that Prospero may believe that language
binds Caliban to him and serves as a limit upon him, an imprison-
ment in the colonizer's system of meanings and enforced social
arrangements, but, as Lamming sees it, that is only one possibility,
and by no means an inevitability. Nor does he embrace cursing as
all that Caliban can do with the tool of language, nor a poeticizing
that testifies to how well he has been assimilated to the master
tongue.[8] Rather, the possession of language for him signifies an
opening towards a futurity which must inevitably change both
Prospero and Caliban. Lamming, who regards Shakespeare as high-
ly as does Greenblatt, refuses to read the play as a species of colonial
mystification, and does not credit the play with a poetic ambiva-
lence that would position Shakespeare somehow above the scene of
his production of the text. Going further than the debunking criti-

William Hogarth's scene from The Tempest *(ca. 1736), the first known illustration of Caliban.*

cism of Prospero which can be found in some recent New Historicist work, Lamming describes Prospero as "an imperialist by circumstance, a sadist by disease; and, above all, an old man in whom envy and revenge are equally matched" (112). Lamming's Prospero is haunted by ingratitude, threatened by the power he unleashes and the opposition he therefore makes possible.

Retamar's acknowledgement of Lamming as a forebearer for his own identification with Caliban serves as the climactic moment in the survey of "Caribbean and African Appropriations of *The Tempest*" that Rob Nixon offered in a 1987 essay that appeared in *Critical Inquiry.*[9] Nixon's essay made his subject available to the Anglo-American academic community; he argues that such appropriations of the play testify to indigenous traditions of writing that are bounded historically by movements of decolonization and nationalization, and that are limited moreover by being an exclusively male tradition of identification with the figure of Caliban. In taking my point of departure from this narrative, I seek to put pressure on these assumptions, and would begin by pursuing some complications that have been overlooked, first by focussing on some terms in Lamming's analysis of his identifications that are ignored in such an account. One place to start is with the psychological emphasis that Lamming gives in the characterization of Prospero that I quoted a moment ago, for, as he stresses, the psychological residue of colonialism remains long after the structure of colonialism, with its founding institution of slavery, has been replaced (albeit with forms of economic domination — or capitulation — neocolonialism, of which Lamming is quite aware[10]); as Lamming put it in an interview:

> the colonial experience is a *live* experience in the *consciousness* of these people. And just because the so-called colonial situation and its institutions may have been transferred into something else, it is a fallacy to think that the human-lived content of those situations are automatically transferred into something else, too. The experience is a continuing *psychic* experience that has to be dealt with and will have to be dealt with long after the actual colonial situation formally "ends."[11]

That residue, however much it may take its origins in the colonial situation, also exceeds it. The situation that Lamming thus describes is not necessarily bounded by colonization, nor does it end with decolonization; this, indeed, is the burden of virtually all of Lamming's novels.

If we return to Retamar's remark about Lamming, a further complication in Lamming's identification with Caliban can be registered in a full citation: "although he is (apparently) the first writer in our world to assume our identification with Caliban, the Barbadian writer George Lamming is unable to break the circle traced by Mannoni" (12). Retamar obviously demurs here from making a full identification with Lamming, and does do by implying that Lamming manifests what Mannoni referred to notoriously

*An 1820 engraving of John Mortimer's 1775 painting
of an animalistic Caliban*

as the dependency complex of the colonized (the notoriety of this claim depends upon its vehement refusal in Frantz Fanon's *Black Skin, White Masks,* but it will have to remain an aside here to note that Mannoni's *Psychologie de la Colonisation* (1950) — translated into English as *Prospero and Caliban* — as well as Fanon's text also might be read as interventions motivated by Shakespeare's play). Retamar's critique, like Nixon's analysis, assumes that identification with Caliban must be total, and must testify to a nativist resistance. Oddly enough, Retamar somehow believes that this can occur through identification with Shakespeare's Caliban — as if that fig-ure were the native. Yet, I think more to the point, and certainly not merely as a sign of dependence, is the situation offered in Lam-ming's reading of *The Tempest,* which takes its founding moment in Caliban's account of his initial relationship with Prospero, the betrayal signaled in the offer of water with berries and the educa-tion that Prospero initiates (1.2.330-44).

> Caliban is his [Prospero's] convert, colonised by lan-guage, and excluded by language. It is precisely this gift of lan-guage, this attempt at transformation which has brought about the pleasure and paradox of Caliban's exile. . . . The gift is a contract from which neither participant is allowed to withdraw. Caliban plots murder against Prospero, not in hatred, and not in fear, but out of a deep sense of betrayal. Prospero threatens Caliban with pain; but he never mentions murder; for he knows that the death of Caliban is the death of an occasion which he needs in order to escape the purgatory which has been crystallised by their encounter. (*Pleasures of Exile* 15)

Lamming certainly does not imagine his Caliban the way Aimé Césaire does in his rewriting of *The Tempest* as *Une Tempête,* where the first word out of his mouth is "Uhuru." Failing to make such an emancipatory gesture of pan-African solidarity, Lamming's text could be seen as not having broken with colonization, but I think it is closer to the point to suggest that he sees that colonization is not yet over. It is the case, moreover, that Lamming does affirm a nativist, peasant, and Africanist position. But it is always complicated by the impure origin of the colonized subject. Caliban is, for Lamming, a relational being, who comes into existence through colonization, through Prospero. Indeed, although one wouldn't know it from an account like Nixon's, which takes his first word to be his last, this is also the case with Césaire, who ends *Une Tempête* with Caliban declining to kill Prospero and locked with him in a dialectical struggle whose outcome remains to be seen.

Although Lamming looks to a future in which "Caliban Orders History," he never forgets the linguistic situation of Caliban and what it signifies. Thus, while it is certainly the case that Lamming "declares himself to be Caliban's heir" as Nixon summarizes his argument (567), he identifies with Prospero as well, a double paternity that Nixon ignores and Retamar implicitly deplores. This double paternity is crucial for me in the reading of these materials that I wish to pursue; here is Lamming's formulation:

> I am a direct descendant of slaves, too near to the actual enterprise to believe that its echoes are over with the reign of emancipation. Moreover, I am a direct descendant of Prospero worshipping in the same temple of endeavour, using his legacy of language — not to curse our meeting — but to push it further, reminding the descendants of both sides that what's done is done, and can only be seen as a soil from which other gifts, or the same gift endowed with different meanings, may grow towards a future which is colonised by our acts in this moment, but which must always remain open. (*Pleasures of Exile* 15)

To begin to take the measure of this gesture, I would recall Lamming's 1960 novel *Season of Adventure,* which has among its protagonists a revolutionary woman in search of her father; it remains undecideable in that text whether her father is white or black. Fola is unavoidably double, and her coming to revolutionary consciousness is formulated in her recognition that she is "Fola and other than Fola, meaning bastard."[12] Bastard: this is also Caliban's condition in Shakespeare's play; his paternity remains unknown, Prospero declares him illegitimate. For Lamming, this is the condition of the colonial subject. Strikingly, in *Season of Adventure,* that subject is not necessarily male, and this suggests that in Lamming the Caliban position — as a position of illegitimacy — cannot be tied to the kind of essentializing of gender that can be found in an account like Nixon's. When Lamming places paternity in doubt by doubling the father, the apparatuses of institutionalized heterosexuality can be put in question. At such a juncture, the colonial subject points, as Lamming suggests, towards a futurity not to be determined by prior determinations. It is this opening that particularly interests me as a place where queer theory and post-colonial interventions may meet.

Lamming provides a limited route to this enterprise; his Fola is an exceptional character.[13] The revolution is thought of as a male domain; as a bastard Fola has a kind of honorary status as one of "The Boys from Forest Reserve, the original and forgotten bastards of the new republic" (*Season of Adventure* 292). Her status can be compared to that of the lesbian Penelope of Lamming's 1958 novel *Of Age and Innocence,* especially as seen in an entry from her diary:

> I shall always feel the mark 'in spite of,' branded on my presence. Penelope in spite of . . . Penelope in spite of . . . It would be better to lose one's status completely and be seen wholly as a new thing; much better than to have one's status granted with a certain reservation. . . . I believe this is what those people who are called inferior experience, and find resentful and intolerable. . . . The Negro, the homosexual, the Jew, the worker . . . he is a man, that is never denied, but he is not quite ready for definition until these reservations are stated, and it is the reservation which separates him from himself. He is a man in spite of . . . I shall be Penelope in spite of. . . .[14]

This passage could be compared to an essay of Lamming's on the condition of being a "Negro" writer, someone inevitably identified within "a category of men called Negro," with the consequence that "the eye which catches and cages him, has seen him as a man, but a man *in spite of. . . .*"[15]

Lamming's position here is a political one that does not seek to launch itself from the platform of identity; yet it also does not seek to deny difference. It might be compared to the climactic moment at the end of his first novel, *In the Castle of My Skin* (1953), a conversation that the protagonist G has with his friend Trumper who has returned to Barbados from the U.S. Trumper plays G a recording of Paul Robeson singing "Go Down Moses" and identifies with the "people" in that spiritual.

> "What people?" [G] ask[s]. . . .
> "My People," said Trumper. . . .
> "Who are your people?" I asked him. It seemed a kind of huge joke.
> "The Negro race," said Trumper.[16]

G is puzzled by this answer; although he understands the racial label he does not know that it applies to him. Trumper explains: "the blacks here are my people too, but they don't know it yet. You don't know it yourself" (*Castle* 295).

Racial identity in this formulation is at once something one might be and yet not know; something that others might know and stigmatize without one even knowing that as the cause of the stigma. It is, moreover, in *The Castle of My Skin,* as in Lamming's essay cited a moment ago, a sign that the supposedly universal liberal subject of rights does not include someone who is a person "in spite of."[17] This explains not only why a character like Penelope, whose lesbian desires are known to no one, experiences her secret as stigma, but also how what D.A. Miller terms the "open secret" structures racial identity in a phobic world; it explains the conflicted state of consciousness that Lamming represents in his alterego G, whose racial identity is a secret to himself but not to those who are responsible for his systematic oppression. This point in Lamming might be said to follow from W.E.B. Du Bois's crucial concept of double consciousness and to echo Fanon's configuration of black skin and white mask.

Lamming's Penelope extends her self-understanding to include "the Negro, the Jew, the homosexual, the worker," and I would want to further the move offered by this conjunction by comparing it to some recent critical interventions in the Caribbean tradition of *The Tempest* represented by Lamming. Penelope does not include in her list the category "women" and while this might be read as a sign of Lamming's limited purchase on questions of gender, it might also be understood in terms provided in a stunningly complex 1990 essay by Sylvia Wynter that attempts, as the title of her essay puts it, to move "Beyond Miranda's Meanings: Un/silencing the 'Demonic Ground' of Caliban's 'Woman.'"[18] Wynter's is one of a number of texts that might be instanced to counter Nixon's claim that *The Tempest* only solicits male identification and thus ceased to be pertinent in colonial struggle once feminists became a strong voice in the Caribbean. For notable, as the title of Wynter's essay might suggest, is her identification with Caliban's 'woman'; that this 'woman' actively rewrites the play is suggested by the fact that Wynter puts 'woman' in scarequotes in part to distinguish Caliban's 'woman' from Miranda. Wynter's is a feminist reading that nonetheless resists the feminist reading of the play that would forge identifications with Miranda. For however much Miranda is Prospero's tool she is also Caliban's accuser and reviler.

Wynter understands the play as an index to a global transformation that begins for her (as for Du Bois[19]) in the Renaissance, one in which racial difference comes to be installed as a categorical difference that overrides gender difference; this is why Miranda's gender is no guarantee of difference in terms of racial positioning. Through the figure of Miranda, Wynter addresses feminist criticism that too easily universalizes a notion of "woman," and which, inevitably, whitens and Europeanizes its subject. She balks, too, at simply describing the culture that produces Miranda as a patriarchal one, insisting that Prospero is not simply her father but also a monarch, and that it is within the spheres of European state con-

An engraving of Henry Fuseli's painting of The Tempest, *commissioned for the Boydell Shakespeare Gallery (1789), in which Prospero faces a thickly muscled but not entirely human Caliban*

solidation and colonial expansion that patriarchy must be repositioned. Thus, for instance, she takes Irigaray to task, presumably for her focus on classical and psychoanalytic texts whose dehistoricized categories of gender are blind to the historical transformation that Wynter seeks to outline. "If, before the sixteenth century, what Irigaray terms as *'patriarchal discourse'* had erected itself on the 'silenced ground' of women, from then on, the new primarily silenced ground . . . would be that of the majority population-groups of the globe" (363). In this formulation, what is noteworthy is the attempt to replace gendered positions with populations, an insistence on Caliban's 'woman' as the answer to the structure of desire in *The Tempest,* where, as Wynter notes, every male character's desire — whether he be a prince, a plebe, or a native — is, as she puts it, "soldered" (361) onto Miranda. Although it might seem, in invoking the figure of Caliban's 'woman' as a "native" alternative to Miranda, that Wynter is merely proposing a racialized and heterosexual population-production, Caliban's 'woman' is a figure for new populations and new ways of thinking, possibilities "beyond the 'master discourse' . . . and its sub/versions. Beyond Miranda's meanings" (366). The orthographic play of the slash in sub/versions expresses Wynter's sense of the complicities of (white) feminism with male/colonial dominance, while the "beyond" here beckons, I think, not at a mere binaristic overturning but towards something genuinely new, perhaps the "wholly new thing" glanced at in Penelope's diary ruminations, or the "different kind of creature" that Trumper explains to G.

I would read Wynter's figure of Caliban's 'woman' alongside the position of identification that Michelle Cliff offers in a 1991 essay titled "Caliban's Daughter: The Tempest and the Teapot."[20] If Wynter writes as "Caliban's 'Woman'," Cliff's title positions herself as "Caliban's Daughter," thus claiming a place within the population that Wynter imagines. Cliff's essay is intent on a search for the mother — indeed, for Cliff, the grandmother as a site of primordial identification — "the forest, . . . Sycorax, the precolonial female" (39) — but its title gestures to the possibility of claiming Caliban as father. The genealogical impulse in Cliff's essay is, even more so than Wynter's, only nominally heterosexual; the paternal gesture seems entirely ancillary to, if not beside the point of Cliff's most pointed identifications with the "old woman." An alternative genealogy is being imagined here, much as Wynter's population-production might also be thought to exceed a simply racialized biologism. For Cliff's "old woman," she writes is "liberated from the feminine role" (even though she is a grandmother) and "may claim masculinity as hers" (47).

Cliff's move — with its potential across gender — provides further pressure on Nixon's claim that "the play's declining pertinence" after the 1970s "has been exacerbated by the difficulty of wresting from it any role for female defiance or leadership" (577). This is not to deny that such texts as Lamming's or Retamar's — or Aimé Césaire's *Une Tempête* — offer very limited affordances for women, although Césaire in fact figures significantly in Cliff's essay both for his delineation of the colonial situation and for the fact that his Caliban claims through Sycorax an identification with nature that cannot be broken. Such moves across gender could perhaps be compared to Lamming's affirmation of double paternity and bastardy, or even to Retamar's argument that our America is a mestizo population.[21] It could be put beside Wynter's insistence that the new population of which Caliban's woman forms a vanguard must embrace those oppressed by class, gender, or "sexual preference" (359); precisely because the modern racial binarism is rooted in notions of biological difference and of the natural, Wynter explicitly calls into question "allegedly 'natural' erotic preference" (365). Thus, in contrast to *The Tempest* which affirms Miranda as the only possible object of desire, Wynter insists on Caliban's 'woman' as offering "an alternative sexual-erotic model of desire" (360).

Wynter does not further develop the possibility that this alternative might include non-heterosexual couplings; Cliff's essay however offers a sustained meditation on these questions. Besides her identification as Caliban's daughter and her insistence on a certain masculinity in the figure of the grandmother — or, on a literary register, her recourse to Césaire — Cliff asks provocatively, as she reviews her childhood reading: "What does it mean when the Jamaican tomboy says, 'I am Heathcliff?' Or finds herself drawn to Bertha when she is told to identify with Jane?" (43-44). The primordial black woman with whom Cliff makes her most profound identification cannot be confined within gendered definitions. Cliff explains the "masculinization" of this figure in a number of ways, as liberation from the "feminine role" in the case of the "old woman" past childbearing years but not beyond serving as an inspiring model for self-relocation. Indeed, Cliff continues, "to be masculine in this context, in the context of the Caribbean, is not to be 'mannish' but to have access to self-definition" (48). But to be masculine also means the ability "to claim that part of the self associated with the nonfeminine, whatever that might be" (48), a hesitation in definition overcome when Cliff points to the ways in which Charlotte Bronte figures Bertha's nonfemininity as masculinity and monstrosity: "I find myself thinking of the notion of the lesbian as monster, marauder; the man/woman in the closet" (48).

Cliff's rewriting of *The Madwoman in the Attic* here is clear, for she continues by considering what female identification with the figure of the black woman entails, what it means "to love another woman — psychically and physically — in the Caribbean landscape" (48). Of some interest here — and certainly a sign that Cliff's thinking moves well beyond the simple posing of analogies offered in Penelope's diary entry, and that it carries further the project represented by Wynter's intervention, is that Cliff has no desire to call what she is describing *lesbian*. That is, she marks that term for sexual arrangements as a particularly western form of female-female sexuality. This serves to dehomogenize notions of homosexuality, to deny universality to such social formations — a belief which almost always assumes that homosexuality western-style is homosexuality *tout court*. Hence Cliff reclaims forms of "native" sexuality that do not fit within normative boundaries, whether they are, in western terms, heterosexual or homosexual. And most explicitly, she repudiates the notion that "one woman loving another woman" only can emblematize "western decadence," that such relations only serve to show "the seduction of the tropics by Europe" (48).

The most powerful image of this demonic ground is conjured up by Cliff in the figure of "Nanny," the Maroon revolutionary reported to have routed the British in Jamaican revolts; she "could catch a bullet between her buttocks and fire the lead back at her attackers. She is the Jamaican Sycorax. The extent to which you can believe in the powers of Nanny, that they are literal examples of her Africanness and strength, represents the extent to which you have

Beerbohm Tree in fur, seaweed, and shells (1904),
painted by Charles A. Buchel

decolonized your mind" (47). That it is Nanny's anus that epitomizes these powers should not be overlooked, for this suggests that it is not biological reproduction that serves to reproduce racial knowledge or self-knowledge. Hence, Cliff's essay arrives at Nanny through a genealogy that proceeds from Sycorax and Caliban to Heathcliff and Bertha Rochester. However much Cliff reclaims nature, she does so in the spirit of a "deconstructivist, wild colonial girl" (42), as she puts it, and the de-essentializing impulses in her essay forge the links that allow for the movement across gender difference, and that recognize conventional gender as western and colonializing. In this respect, Cliff's Nanny could be compared to a moment late in Lamming's *Castle of My Skin,* G's last night on Barbados before he emigrates. He visits a prostitute, but rather than having sex, he tells her a story about two boys, one of whom gives the other a shit-smeared stick. G can't stay to explain the story's meaning to the prostitute (or to the novel's reader), but he has meditated just a moment before about what is hidden in the castle of his skin; the story posits an eroticized — and stigmatized — connection between boys. G tells the prostitute the story, withholds sex and meaning from her. This marks a limit overcome by Cliff's Nanny, returning bullets shot from her buttocks.

This would be an appropriate point, I think, to return to Lamming's discussion of *The Tempest* in *Pleasures of Exile,* to note how it moves from considerations of the linguistic tie of Prospero and Caliban to confront the charge that Caliban desired to rape Miranda.[22] For it is this accusation that should form the stumbling block in any easy appropriation of Caliban as a point of identification, and it is remarkable that a survey like Nixon's never notices that this moment is under scrutiny in a number of texts, Césaire's included. Lamming explicitly labels the charge of attempted rape as "the Lie" (102), capitalizing the term. However, he also credits Caliban's response, "would't had been done," as infused with political meaning. "He does not wish it for the mere experiment of mounting a piece of white pussy," Lamming writes (a stinging answer to the soldering of desire that Wynter notes, as if the only form of male desire would be embodied in a white woman, although also a disturbing way to formulate that position, however much "pussy" may be a West Indian idiom); Lamming values the moment for the fact that Caliban "goes further and imagines that the consequence of such intercourse would be a fabulous increase of the population" (102). While he wonders why Caliban thinks such populations would be Calibans, and insists on acknowledging Miranda's role — "these children would be bastards and should be honoured no less with their mother's name" [102] — he writes, and this echoes his aim in *Season of Adventure* to delegitimate the name of the father and elevate the vilified mother, his thought moves towards the new population of "brown skin" offspring as representing the real threat of the rape. Miranda is either forgotten here, or, as the brainwashed subject of Prospero, as Lamming explicitly portrays her, as complicitous in her dreams of sex with Caliban as Prospero is in making the charge of attempted rape. The charge, thereby, ultimately points for Lamming at Prospero's conception of Caliban, and the horror of miscegenation is seen to lie behind the accusation. Lamming's analysis makes the attempted rape a sign of a structural parallel between Miranda and Caliban, the fact that thanks to Prospero they are "alike in their ignorance" (112). The brown baby is taken as something that would be *theirs:* the result and expression of some fusion both physical and other than physical: a fusion which, within himself, Prospero needs and dreads!" (102).

Lamming goes no further in opening up this dreaded need, although the point reiterates his earlier claim that "Caliban haunts [Prospero] in a way that is almost too deep and too intimate to communicate" (99). The elision of Miranda, and of gendered violence in this analysis, translates the question of rape into a psychological principle of male-male, colonizer/colonized relations. If it is the lie that tells us about Prospero's desires (incest, for instance), it could be said also to be central to the figure — Lamming himself — who declared himself to be the offspring of both Prospero and Caliban. Miranda is erased, made to serve as the supplement of the woman who figures the sexual relationship between men and the productive possibility of men-making-men. Bastardy and mixed-race offspring (along with the violence of rape) serve as the explicit forms for this illegitimate desire of doubled paternity. Language and some primordial Law are invoked as another name for this male-male relationship: "This gift of Language is the deepest and the most delicate bond of involvement. It has a certain finality.

Caliban will never be the same again. Nor, for that matter, will Prospero" (109). This irreversible futurity is figured as the half-breed bastard produced by this indissoluable "bond," a figure hyphenated when Lamming refers to the composite "Prospero-Caliban." In short, the story that Lamming all but tells about the relationship with Prospero is one about the "betrayal of love" (114), a love that dares not speak its name. Or, rather does, in lines spoken by Caliban, Lamming's final citation from *The Tempest*:

> When thou cam'st first,
> Thou strok'dst me, and made much of me; wouldst give me
> Water with berries in't; and teach me how
> To name the bigger light, and how the less,
> That burn by day and night: and then I loved thee.
>
> (1.2. 332-36; as cited in *Pleasures of Exile* 117)

This passage in fact provides Lamming with a title for his 1971 novel *Water With Berries*, a rewriting of *The Tempest* in which the Prospero position is taken, however, by his wife; in this rewriting the Miranda figure, named Myra, is a bastard (she is the daughter of Prospero's brother, Fernando); the revolt that brings down Prospero is enacted on her body in a scene of rape and bestiality, narrated late in the novel by Fernando:

> Perhaps you can imagine how they made the hounds violate her sex. The animals. The very creatures which had been her fondest pets. Those monsters stirred up the animals' lust for her; and let them loose over her body. Just as they had seen their master do with some of them. His own field servants. Oh, yes, my brother, come from the same blessed loins, the same privilege and blood; my brother himself had made this devil's crime a common sport upon his servants. Male and female alike. Trained his hounds to mount a human sex. That monster.[23]

The "monstrous" natives repeat the "monstrosity" of Prospero; as he had made them, male and female, submit to the "devil's crime"

David Suchet as Caliban
(Stratford, 1978)

of bestiality/sodomy, so they unleash the dogs on Myra. The scene reeks of sado-masochistic pleasures, plays out Prospero's sexual fantasies.[24] In presenting the secret of Prospero's desires in this scene, the abjection of such desires as monstrous cannot be separated from the terrifying appeal of untoward couplings, hybrids, border violations. The scene traces the circuits of monstrous contact that circulate through the body of the violated woman who serves as the conduit joining Prospero, his brother, and the natives. Here Prospero/Caliban are one, monstrously alike. This monstrosity is arguably the flip side of futurity, of new possibilities and new populations, a world where fathers are indeterminable, in which female desire rather than bounded by marriage realizes itself in promiscuity, bastard-production, or the lesbianism of Penelope. In these ways Lamming imagines the generation of Caliban outside of the normative modes of social/sexual reproduction. If Caliban was born in the relationship with Prospero, made in abjection, bondage and slavery, the future cannot simply reclaim a time before colonialism, nor its simple reversal, but a reordering which, from the point of view of colonial powers, must appear as the very refusal of the terms of colonial order and a rejection of the abjection and stigma which it places on alternatives. In Lamming these alternative social and sexual arrangements follow from the union of Prospero and Caliban, and are manifest in the Secret Gathering of The Boys, or the even more secreted lines of identification with figurations of aberrant female sexuality.

It is for these reasons that I think it possible to read Lamming alongside Cliff and Wynter. It is also possible to think of him beside an author ignored in the usual surveys of *Tempest* appropriations and rewritings. I have in mind Toni Morrison's 1981 novel *Tar Baby* which is, among other things, a rewriting of *The Tempest*. (Gloria Naylor's *Mama Day* should also be mentioned in this context.) In the central plot device in Morrison's novel, the Prospero figure Valerian and his wife Margaret anticipate the Christmas visit of their son. He fails to arrive; instead an intruder appears in their house, a black man named Son. The plot doubles these two sons, and Valerian is shown ultimately to be responsible both for his wife's abuse and torture of their son as he is for his capitalist participation in exploitations that have their root in slavery and that have produced the immiseration of the black Son. The doubling of sons is further doubled in Morrison's plot through the tense relationships between Son, who represents an unassimilated Africanism, and Jadine, the protegé of Valerian, a black woman who has been thoroughly Europeanized. Morrison's plot plays out a failed romance between Son and Jadine — a romance tinged in its inception by the threat of rape. Son and Jadine are Morrison's Caliban and Miranda. Hers is a heterosexualized version of the tense duplicities of a plot that suggests, like Lamming's, that there can be no easy return to a singularity after the depradations of colonialism. *Tar Baby* thereby indicates that essentialized notions of racial or gendered identity are problematic; it is in that space of problematization that one can also hope for new futures in our America.

Caliban

This tongue that I have mastered
has mastered me;

has taught me curses
in the language of the master

has taught me bondage
in the language of the master

I speak this dispossession
in the language of the master

Abena P.A. Busia, Testimonies of Exile *(1990)*

ENDNOTES

1. See Jonathan Goldberg, "Under the Covers with Caliban," in *Margins of the Text,* ed. D.C. Greetham (Ann Arbor: University of Michigan Press, 1997), pp. 105-28.

2. This prevailing view is documented and critiqued by David Scott Kastan, *Shakespeare after Theory* (New York: Routledge, 1999), "'The Duke of Milan/ And his Brave Son': Old Histories and New in *The Tempest,*" pp. 183-97. In arguing for the primacy of "old world" implications in the play, Kastan ignores the exacting demonstration in Peter Hulme's *Colonial Encounters: Europe and the Native Caribbean, 1492-1797* (London: Routledge, 1986), ch. 3, "Prospero and Caliban," of the ways in which the play is crossed by old world and new world histories, each of which serves as an alibi and complication of the other. On this point, as well as support for the prevailing view, see Peter Hulme and William H. Sherman, ed., *The Tempest and its Travels* (London: Reaktion, 2000).

3. For some Renaissance critics aware of this work, see, e.g., Ania Loomba, *Gender, Race, Renaissance Drama* (Manchester: Manchester University Press, 1989), ch. 6, "Seizing the Book"; Denise Albanese, *New Science, New World* (Durham: Duke University Press, 1996), ch. 2, "Admiring Miranda and Enslaving Nature," n. 23; Jyotsna G. Singh, "Caliban versus Miranda: Race and Gender Conflicts in Post-colonial Rewritings of *The Tempest,*" in *Feminist Readings of Early Modern Culture,* ed. Valerie Traub, M. Lindsay Kaplan and Dympna Callaghan (Cambridge: Cambridge University Press, 1996), pp. 191-209; Richard Halpern, *Shakespeare Among the Moderns* (Ithaca: Cornell University Press, 1997), ch. 2, "Shakespeare in the Tropics," p. 46; "'The picture of Nobody': White Cannibalism in *The Tempest,*" in *The Production of English Renaissance Culture,* ed. D.L. Miller, S. O'Dair and H. Weber (Ithaca: Cornell University Press, 1994), pp. 262-92.

4. Roberto Fernández Retamar, *Caliban and Other Essays,* tr. Edward Baker (Minneapolis: University of Minnesota Press, 1989), p. 12.

5. All citations, unless otherwise noted, are from the reprint of *The Pleasures of Exile* (Ann Arbor: University of Michigan Press, 1992). For an exacting study of the place of Lamming in post-colonial uses of *The Tempest,* see Peter Hulme, "Reading from Elsewhere: George Lamming and the Paradox of Exile," in Hulme and Sherman, ed., *The Tempest and Its Travels,* pp. 220-35.

6. In *First Images of America,* ed. Fredi Chiapelli (Berkeley & Los Angeles: University of California Press, 1976), pp. 561-80.

[7] Paul Brown, "'This thing of darkness I acknowledge mine': *The Tempest* and the discourse of colonialism," in Jonathan Dollimore and Alan Sinfield, ed., *Political Shakespeare* (Ithaca: Cornell University Press, 1985), p. 66.

[8] In "Caliban," the first poem in Abena P.A. Busia's *Testimonies of Exile* (Trenton, N.J.: Africa World Press, 1990), the position of mastery of and by language is deftly handled, indeed in ways that go beyond the stranglehold of the master-tongue that illustrates the poem. It is perhaps noteworthy, in terms of the kinds of identifications that I discuss later in this essay, that Busia follows this initial poem with an untitled poem that begins "and I am a woman ravished and naked" (p. 5), inviting the reader to consider the possibility that it is also spoken in Caliban's voice — or that the author has been speaking as Caliban to begin the sequence. The possibility of a Caliban gendered female is, however, what Suniti Namjoshi offers in her extraordinary sequence, "Snapshots of Caliban," in *Because of India* (London: Only Women Press, 1989). For critical evaluations of her accomplishment, see Diana Brydon, "Sister Letters: Miranda's *Tempest* in Canada," in Marianne Novy, *Cross-Cultural Performances: Differences in Women's Re-Visions of Shakespeare* (Urbana: University of Illinois Press, 1993), pp. 165-84, and Kate Chedgzoy, *Shakespeare's Queer Children* (Manchester: Manchester University Press, 1995), ch. 3, "Rewriting the Narrative of Shame: Women's Transformations of *The Tempest*."

[9] Rob Nixon, "Caribbean and African Appropriations of *The Tempest*," *Critical Inquiry 13* (Spring 1987): 557-78. Nixon's essay considers O. Mannoni's *Prospero and Caliban* (Ann Arbor: University of Michigan Press, 1990), Aimé Césaire's *Une Tempête* (Paris: Seuil, 1969), Lamming, and Retamar, the theorist who receives Nixon's warmest approval; for a broader, if much less politically acute survey, see Alden T. Vaughan and Virginia Mason Vaughan, *Shakespeare's Caliban* (Cambridge: Cambridge University Press, 1991), ch. 6, "Colonial Metaphors," pp. 144-71.

[10] For a stunning and sustained political analysis of the situation of the Caribbean, see Lamming's 1981 address to the Jamaican Press Association reprinted as an appendix in Ambroise Kom, *George Lamming et le destin des Caraibes* (Ville de la Salle, Quebec: Didier, 1986), pp. 263-73, included as well in the speeches and discussions collected in *Conversations: Essays, Addresses, Interviews, 1953-1990*, ed. Richard Drayton and Andaiye (London: Karia Press, 1992), as well as the telling analysis in Lamming's brief "Introduction to 1984 edition" of *The Pleasures of Exile* (London: Allison and Busby, 1984), pp. 6-8. For a reading of Lamming always alert to his understanding of neocolonialism, see Supriya Nair, *Caliban's Curse: George Lamming and the Revisioning of History* (Ann Arbor: University of Michigan Press, 1996).

[11] George E. Kent, "Caribbean Novelist," *Black World* 22.5 (March 1974), p. 92. This citation is the starting point for Peter Hulme's analysis of the psychology of

(neo)colonialism in "The Profit of Language: George Lamming and the Postcolonial Novel," in Jonathan White, ed., *Recasting the World* (Baltimore: Johns Hopkins University Press, 1993), pp. 120-36.

[12] George Lamming, *Season of Adventure* (London: Allison & Busby, 1979), p. 174.

[13] The limited affordances for women in Lamming's texts, and the limitations in his capacity to think about gendered difference, is frequently remarked by Lamming's critics, including Supriya Nair and Sandra Pouchet Paquet, *The Novels of George Lamming* (London: Heinemann, 1982).

[14] George Lamming, *Of Age and Innocence* (London: Allison & Busby, 1981), p. 151.

[15] George Lamming, "The Negro Writer and His World," *Presence Africaine* 18/19 (1956), p. 321.

[16] George Lamming, *In the Castle of My Skin* (Ann Arbor: University of Michigan Press, 1991), p. 295.

[17] In "'A Different Kind of Creature': Caribbean Literature, The Cyclops Factor, and the Second Poetics of the Propter Nos," *Annals of Scholarship* 12.1-2 (1997): 153-72, Sylvia Wynter takes her title phrase from Trumper's dialogue with G to argue that the alterity represented by "the Negro" cannot be assimilated to a Eurocentric same.

[18] The essay appears as the "Afterword" in *Out of the Kumbla: Caribbean Women and Literature,* ed. Carole Boyce Davies and Elaine Savory Fido (Trenton: Africa World Press, 1990). Natasha Barnes worries the question of Wynter's opposition to feminism in "Reluctant Matriarch: Sylvia Wynter and the Problematics of Caribbean Feminism," *Small Axe 5* (March 1999): 34-47, arguing that "Wynter's conclusions lead to a repudiation of feminism as a site of emancipatory imagining" (p. 41). While I do not agree with this reading of Wynter (and am grateful to Prof. Barnes for some stimulating discussion of these issues), it is certainly possible to understand Wynter this way, with damaging effects on feminism; see also Paget Henry's discussion/evaluation of Wynter in *Caliban's Reason* (New York: Routledge, 2000), ch. 5, "Sylvia Wynter: Poststructuralism and Postcolonial Thought," pp. 117-43, which barely mentions questions of gender in drawing its assessments of Wynter's thought.

[19] See W.E.B. Du Bois, "The Development of a People," in *Writings,* ed. Herbert Aptheker (Millwood, N.Y.: Kraus-Thomson Organization Ltd., 1982), i: 201-15, and the concise and stunning sentence on p. 207: "The African Slave trade was the child of the Renaissance." My thanks to Nahum D. Chandler for drawing this text to my attention. Wynter elaborates the model of social transformation in her "Afterword" in "A Different Kind of Creature" as well as in such essays as: "1492: A New World View," in Vera Lawrence Hyatt and Rex Nettleford, ed., *Race, Discourse, and the Origin of the Americas: A New World View* (Washington, D.C.: Smithsonian Institution Press, 1995), pp. 5-57; "Columbus, the Ocean Blue, and Fables That Stir the Mind: To Reinvent the Study of Letters," in

Bainard Cowan and Jefferson Humphries, ed., *Poetics of the Americas: Race, Founding, and Textuality* (Baton Rouge: Louisiana State University Press, 1997), pp. 141-63.

[20] Michelle Cliff, "Caliban's Daughter: The Tempest and the Teapot," *Frontiers* 12.2 (1991): 36-51; this essay exists in a number of forms. The earliest version I know is "Clare Savage as a Crossroads Character," in Selwyn R. Cudjoe, *Caribbean Women Writers* (Wellesley/ Amherst: Calaloux/ University of Massachusetts Press, 1990), pp. 263-68, its most recent recension, "Caliban's Daughter or Into the Interior," *American Visions/ Visiones de las Americas* (1994): 152-59.

[21] That is, once the masculinist and homophobic biases of Retamar's text are confronted; on this, see Ricardo L. Ortiz, "Revolution's Other Histories: The Sexual, Cultural, and Critical Legacies of Roberto Fernández Retamar's 'Caliban,'" *Social Text* 58 (1999): 33-58.

[22] Chantal Zabus, "A Calibanic Tempest in Anglophone and Francophone New World Writing," *Canadian Literature* 104 (1985): 35-50, makes this point, but considerably simplifies Lamming's texts by treating both acts as instances of the violence of the colonizer, as the two principal weapons "of the colonizer's arsenal" (39).

[23] George Lamming, *Water with Berries* (New York: Holt, Rinehart and Winston, 1971), p. 228.

[24] To treat this scene as revealing Prospero's incestuous desire for his daughter, as Kom does, *George Lamming et le destin des Caraibes,* p. 96, and as Hulme does too, "The Profit of Language," pp. 127-29, ignores all the other forms of "aberrant" sexuality here.

ABOUT THE AUTHOR

 JONATHAN GOLDBERG is Sir William Osler Professor of English Literature at The Johns Hopkins University, where he has taught since 1986. He has also held positions at Temple University, Brown University and Duke University. The past recipient of awards from the American Philosophical Society, the American Council of Learned Societies, and the John Simon Guggenheim Memorial Foundation, he has been a fellow at the Humanities Research Center at The Australian National University and in 2001-02 will be a fellow at the Center for the Critical Analysis of Contemporary Culture at Rutgers University.

Goldberg is the author of seven books: *Endlesse Worke: Spenser and the Structures of Discourse* (Johns Hopkins University Press, 1981); *James I and The Politics of Literature: Jonson, Shakespeare, Donne and Their Contemporaries* (Johns Hopkins University Press, 1983); *Voice Terminal Echo: Postmodernism and English Renaissance Texts* (Methuen, 1986); *Writing Matter: From the Hands of the English Renaissance* (Stanford University Press, 1990); *Sodometries: Renaissance Texts, Modern Sexualities* (Stanford University Press, 1992); *Desiring Women Writing: English Renaissance Examples* (Stanford University Press, 1997) and *Willa Cather and Others* (Duke University Press, 2001). With Stephen Orgel, he coedited Milton for the Oxford Authors edition and for Oxford World's Classics. He is also editor of *Queering the Renaissance* (Duke University Press, 1994) and *Reclaiming Sodom* (Routledge, 1994).

His 2001 Garnett Sedgewick Memorial Lecture forms part of a larger book project on *The Tempest* and its anti-colonial rewritings and repositionings in twentieth-century Afro-Caribbean texts. As in a number of his earlier books, Goldberg aims in this project to articulate relationships between early modernity and the present. In particular, he seeks to trace connections between early and recent formulations of race, gender, and sexuality towards an understanding of the new kinds of persons generated by the colonial experience.